My Fourth of July

Lorraine Harrison

Infomax Readers

Rosen Classroom™

New York

Published in 2013 by The Rosen Publishing Group, Inc.
29 East 21st Street, New York, NY 10010

Book Design: Katelyn Londino

Photo Credits: Cover © iStockphoto.com/Veni; p. 4 © iStockphoto.com/Yarinca; p. 5 Samuel Acosta/Shutterstock.com; p. 6 Morgan Lane Photography/Shutterstock.com; p. 7 commons.wikimedia.org/wiki/File:Declaration_independence.jpg/Wikipedia.org; p. 8 commons.wikimedia.org/wiki/File:BattleofLongisland.jpg/Wikipedia.org; p. 9 Steve Cole/Vetta/Getty Images; p. 10 © iStockphoto.com/kali9; pp. 11, 16 iStockphoto/Thinkstock.com; pp. 12, 13, 14 Vsevolod33/Shutterstock.com; p. 15 Purestock/Thinkstock.com; p. 17 © iStockphoto.com/adlifemarketing; p. 18 redswept/Shutterstock.com; p. 19 Craig Hanson/Shutterstock.com; p. 20 GWImages/Shutterstock.com; p. 21 Jami Garrison/Shutterstock.com.

ISBN: 978-1-4488-9046-0
6-pack ISBN: 978-1-4488-9047-7

Manufactured in the United States of America

CPSIA Compliance Information: Batch #WS12RC: For further information contact Rosen Publishing, New York, New York at 1-800-237-9932.

Word Count: 402

Contents

America's Birthday

I love holidays! I **celebrate** holidays with my family. We like to celebrate the Fourth of July. It's a very special day.

The Fourth of July is also called Independence Day. "Independence" means **freedom**. This day celebrates America's birthday. We honor our country on this day.

A Free Country

We celebrate America's freedom on the Fourth of July. America wasn't always a free country. It was once ruled by England.

On July 4, 1776, Americans told the world that they wanted to be free. This is why the Fourth of July is America's birthday.

America went to war with England to win its freedom.

America won the war! It became a free country.

There are many ways to celebrate America's freedom. My family and I always do lots of fun things on the Fourth of July!

Celebrating Outside

The Fourth of July is during the summer. The weather is hot and sunny. My family and I spend lots of time outside on the Fourth of July.

We see lots of American flags on the Fourth of July. The American flag is red, white, and blue. I count 50 stars on the flag.

A Big Parade

My family and I go to a big **parade**. We see a marching band in the parade. The band plays loud music.

I know the songs the band plays. They're songs about America. I like to sing these songs. They say good things about our country.

The band plays our national anthem. This is a song that stands for our country. Many people sing this song at the parade.

Fourth of July Foods

After the parade, we go to a party at my Aunt Sue's house. I see my **cousins**. We play outside together.

Aunt Sue is a good cook. She cooks hot dogs outside.

I love to eat hot dogs. They're my **favorite** food!

My mom makes dessert for us to eat after dinner.

She bakes an apple pie. We eat it with ice cream!

Fireworks!

When dinner is done, we walk to the park. We watch fireworks at the park. Many other people we know are there, too.

Fireworks are very loud! They're also bright and colorful. I see red and blue fireworks in the sky.

A Special Holiday

I love to celebrate the Fourth of July. It's fun to honor my country's birthday. It makes me feel proud to be an American.

The Fourth of July is a fun holiday to celebrate.

What do you do to celebrate America's birthday?

A Fun Fourth of July

What do I do on the Fourth of July?

go to a party

eat apple pie with ice cream

play with my cousins

eat hot dogs

watch fireworks

watch a parade

sing the national anthem

see a marching band

Glossary

celebrate (SEH-luh-brayt) To do special things for a holiday or other important day.

cousin (KUH-zuhn) The child of a person's aunt and uncle.

favorite (FAY-vuh-ruht) Liked best.

freedom (FREE-duhm) When a person or group is free.

parade (puh-RAYD) An event where people march in the streets and bands play music.

Index